STEPPING
INTO
BRILLIANT AIR

COLIN OLIVER

The Shollond Trust
London

Published in 2020 by The Shollond Trust.
87B Cazenove Road, London N16 6BB, England
www.headless.org
headexchange@gn.apc.org

Interior design: Richard Lang
Cover design: rangsgraphics.com

The Shollond Trust is a UK charity reg. No 1059551

ISBN: 978-1-908774-76-7

Acknowledgements
This book is made up of poems and prose pieces written between 1967
and 1999. It includes poems from three collections:

In The Open (Shollond Publications, 1974)
Seeing (Interim Press, 1980)
and Speaking Trees (Downstream Press, 1999).

Grateful acknowledgements are due to the editors of the following
publications in which a number of the uncollected poems first appeared:

Iron, Lines Review, Memes, The Middle Way,
The Mountain Path, Blithe Spirit, and Share It.

My special thanks go to Richard Lang of The Shollond Trust
for his inspiration and patience.

Also by Colin Oliver:
Incredible Countries: a gathering of poems.

STEPPING
INTO
BRILLIANT AIR

CONTENTS

In The Open (1974)

for Douglas

Bees

To the orchard
we take the new hive
and put on our veiled hats.

The swarm hangs
among the apple blossom.
Down they drop

with one shake
of the branch –
half a bucket of bees!

Poured into the hive
they quieten
to the drip of syrup.

Watching,
I'm a veiled hat
with nobody inside.

Evening

Stopped on the path to listen
to a warbler in the reeds,
between myself and these
reeds, stones, dry cracks in the earth,
there is no distance:
I have become seeing.
Overhead a plane circles,
lights winking, and goes.

Wolf

World I am you;
I cannot be kept at bay.
A wolf, I take all
in one bite.

My features have become
nothing but mouth,
a mouth nothing but air.

Here on the plain
of openness
I am ever new to myself.

And the world before me
is like a forest
on which suddenly
snow has fallen.

Cold Mountain

(After Han Shan)

1
When I came to Cold Mountain
I made my home among pines
at the foot of a green cliff.
Yet who is here? Cold Mountain:
a vacant house. Jagged peaks,
white clouds and crying monkeys.

2
After a shower rocks gleam
and Cold Mountain from high peak
down to green border shimmers.
I wander by a clear stream,
watch pebbles in the water,
slip about on the wet moss.

3

In a valley where mist hangs
I sit by a rock, stay clear,
and see no inside or out.
At sunset, arriving home,
I stretch and take off my cap,
find it beaded with moisture.

4

I fetch water from the pool
where the herons fish; I share
the mountain fruit with monkeys.
At the centre I have found
a jewel and gained nothing.
The wind hums in the pine trees.

At The Bridge

On the way home I stop
at the bridge, the river
rising as the snow thaws.
I am transparent: here
only water, and on
the castle mound the stone
wall like an animal
peering across white fields.

Seven Haiku

In honeysuckle
    over the blackbird's nest
        the mother's eye.

Here I see no-one
    to cast, on the petals of
        this rose, this shadow.

The pavement shattered
    into hundreds of pieces –
        sudden fall of rain.

Puddles are windows –
    through them we see the clouds that
        pass beneath the road.

The delight I feel
    goes stamping up the road in
        the little boy's coat.

On this road
    only my torchlight moves
        this winter night.

Rain falls to my face –
    a streetlight is reflected
        on the road surface.

Air

1
Being air and formless
but for hands scattering
breadcrumbs, and these sparrows
on the path, I wonder:
who gives here, who receives?

2
Where the road deepens
I lean on the bank
and watch geese flying over.
In this same air
my thoughts pass,
inside and out become one.

3
Distress, for this heart,
is in my being set apart
in bones and flesh:
its release in my being
everyone's eye, and seeing
not one thing outside.

Late Afternoon

Late afternoon, the rain passed, I go out
to post a letter. Leaves on the chestnut
lift in the wind. Nothing but this moment:
my hand lifts, the mouth of the box drips rain.

Seven Sayings

(After the Gnostic Gospel of Thomas)

1
Jesus said:
>The seeker must not fall
>until he finds;
>and when he finds he will fall
>and when he falls
>he will be raised into wonder.

2
And he said:
>Within the body
>a vast treasure is hidden,
>and this is a great wonder.

3
Jesus said:
>I will show you
>>what is seen without eyes,
>>heard without ears.
>I will show you
>>what hand has not touched,
>>hidden in the heart of man.

4

His disciples asked:

> Tell us, when will the truth appear?

Jesus replied:

> When, like little children,
> you let your appearance drop
> like clothes at your feet.
> Then will the Living One appear.

5

Jesus was asked if he came from the One.
He replied:

> I came from that which is steady
> and to that I return.

And he said:

> When veiled it is full of darkness,
> when unveiled it is full of light.

6

Jesus said:

>Blessed is he who is open,
>for the world is within him.

7

And Jesus said:

>He who drinks from my mouth
>becomes me
>and I become him,
>>and to him the secrets are revealed.

Thought-Bees

If thoughts were bees,
who would dare to shut them
tight in the hive of the head?

He who shatters
this hive of pretence
with the swift hammer of seeing,

sees no box, no house,
no door to lock.
The spell of images is broken

and the swarm
breaks out
to scatter in the world.

The hive of nothingness
brings to the world
the honey of love,

and thought-bees,
watched by the queen
of the eye, roam free.

Peeling Potatoes

This morning, after rain
had cleared the air, sparrows
ranged over the cornfield.
I stood at the window
in the kitchen where now
I peel these potatoes.
They come white from the knife,
roll into the water.
I am clear and look down
as if from a window.

Sea Shell

What secret lies
in the heart of a sea shell
you cannot tell.

But if one day
a shell on a rock should crack
and break its back

your gaze may fall
to find in its secret heart
nothing at all.

Then turning round
to the sea you may wonder
that the waves' sound

can come from an empty heart.

Visiting Friends

A hedge wild with hawthorn,
bramble, dog rose,
dogwood, wild hop and old man's beard.
We walked down to see it
and share now both view
and the eye that sees.

The river is dry,
rugged with hoof marks.
Flints in the bank were once heated
to drop in water skins.
Feather in hand, my son
stumbles after
a chicken that will not keep still.

Love

(After Kabir)

Kabir says: I will tell you
    the secret of love.
The weaver does not weave it,
    nor is it grown in the fields,
    yet love is for sale in the market.
Go there now: king or beggar,
    anyone can afford it,
    your money stays in your pocket.
What do you exchange for love?
Kabir says: lose no time,
    cut off your head
    and take love in return.

Peace

is the station
where one waits
but with nowhere to go
and where

the grain
of a bench runs
like rails through
incredible countries.

Endpoem

(For Vivian)

Given to God,
     the worn sandals of thought
     left at a distant threshold,
one's care is for Him alone
that His care may be for all.

Before Him, in His mystery,
the unclenching
of the fists of knowing –
     the unhanding of all things to Him,
     being in oneself nothing
     and no-one,
     the fool with open palms –
before Him, that one
might happily contain Him.

Being empty and light,
one is God, His all and His love,
held within the light –
     and one sinks as the light
     to God, through God and,
     for His sake, beyond God.

One is
a pebble turned between God's fingers
to be tossed
into the pool of His everlasting clearness
     that His hand might be free.

The Light-Man And
The Rainbow

The Light-Man And The Rainbow

At the edge of the cornfield a man sheltered from the rain. He looked up at the lime tree under which he stood and watched its leaves shimmering. His shirt was spotted with wet patches which were slowly drying as he waited for the shower to pass.

In the sky that could be seen through the leaves a rainbow appeared. The man walked from under the tree to get a clear view of the sky. In the west the sun was shining as the shower clouds moved eastwards. Against a background of grey cloud in the east the rainbow stood full and radiant. It rose from behind the village church to the left of the man, arched through the sky high above the fields and descended behind a line of trees. The rain was still falling as the man stood and watched the rainbow.

When he was a child, he remembered, the sight of a rainbow would make him wish that he could fly like a bird. There were times when he tried to take off, using his arms as wings and half believing that he might be given the power to rise. The fact that other people couldn't fly need not prevent him from discovering his own special gift.

If he could fly he would go to the end of the rainbow, reaching it before it faded. He had imagined not a crock of gold at the rainbow's end but a casket with a secret treasure.

His wish had been long forgotten. But as he remembered it and thought of what he had recently discovered, it occurred to him that his wish had in a sense come true.

The light rain which had been falling through the sunlight stopped. The sky above the man became blue but the rainbow still held.

A seagull appeared in the sky, white against the blue,

flying slowly towards the broken sheet of cloud. The man shielded his eyes against the sunlight with his hand and watched the seagull. He was filled with light and there was nothing to keep the light shut in. He saw that he could fly, not as a man, but as the bird that he was watching. He saw that he was the seagull. His self was the air, the container of all things, and all that he contained he was.

The seagull was a white speck in the distance, the rainbow was fading in the sunlight. The man looked at the trees where the rainbow came down. He was there at the rainbow's end.

Nobody Here

A Ship's Hull

A ship's hull,
its figurehead severed and lost,
lies at the shore of your absence.

The diver of your eye
has discovered
the pearl of your being

and you hold it,
as you would a lantern
on a starless night.

It is within you and within all things –
it is the island's beacon,
the lime of voyages –

and your line is cast
not to things
but to that which is ever yours,

their inmost nature.

Light

The interior light
is nothing but light;
light upon light.

It is a still pool.
Fingers that try to touch
will, without a ripple, disappear.

The interior light
is the clear light of being.
The light on the rock.

Close to, the eye
may catch the swing
of the lamp of amazement,

but the light itself
is nothing but light;
light upon light.

Nobody Here

In the striving
to grow into non-existence
there come
    the seasons of perfection:

moments when the already present,
absolute in its clearness,
consumes
    any hint of human presence:

there is nobody here at all.

When seeing becomes perfect being
what occurs is not
    all that I see I am,
but everything is eyeing its own appearance –

and the pebble in the air
is one
with the hand that has thrown it,

for all things are being themselves in me.

Become Nothing

(After Ansari)

Who walks on water
is no better than a straw.
Who flies in the air
is no better than a fly.
Be without equal:
become nothing.
Find the real self
where no self exists.
The heart resigns
and the eye sees
nothing but God.

The Smallest Thing

If I am nothing
the smallest thing
a blade of grass
a spider on my arm
an owl slowly passing
becomes a gift.

The Blue Chair

The blue chair
by the window:
we wonder that it is.

The chair, the lamp,
the glass vase –
all just there.

Starfish
in the desert,
how is it that they are?

They speak
with quiet insistance:
being is happening.

Why they don't crumble
into dust, into less than dust,
we'll never know.

As a man on a windy day
holds on to his hat,
being holds on to itself.

Rumi

To the fires of non-existence,
you, like a moth to the candle's flame,
were drawn. Your eyes,
as the eyes on wings, became light
and in that light were one.

Your face was the Sun of Tabriz.
Like Icarus you flew
but you had nowhere to fall.
Your ocean was the ocean of invisibility;
you plucked there a wealth of sea-roses
and gave each one the name of love.

O Rumi, without ears you held
the notes of the reed-flute within you;
bodiless, you were all your spinning dancers.
With no tongue you spoke
and poems leapt like porpoises
from the waters of your being.

Beheaded, you were the light
that is the heart of your Beloved.
Utterly poor, you found His world
to be your own. For you,
there could be no 'I' and 'thou'.

Twelve Notes
On The Track Of God

Twelve Notes on the Track of God

Secretly nature seeks and hunts and tries
to ferret out the track in which God
may be found.

Meister Eckhart.

1

I can know so much about surfaces, but so little
about what lies underneath, and how true this
is of myself. As I grew, I lost sight of my real
nature. I lived outside myself, on the outside of
everything: unable to mention one thing not a
closed door to me. This was the deepest cause of
my distress.

What do I find if I look inside myself? My
outside look and my inside look are as different as
earth and air. If I turn to the inside, open this one
door, I see into my own nothingness. This seeing
is the one work I can call my own.

2

Just as bees can probe into flowers, we can
see into ourselves. Bees discover nectar, we
discover God.

We are blessed because God, being simple, can
be known. Nothing is simpler than our own
nothingness, and this is the root of God.

3

To see our real nature we must assume nothing
and just look. We must give up knowledge and
become ignorant, give up understanding and
become foolish.

4

The path by which I take leave of God is called imagination, and I become a somebody. The path by which I approach God is called seeing, and I become a nobody. If I entertain the least image of myself, I mask the truth. If I turn inwards, I find myself stripped of all appearances.

5

It's strange, but when I move into God and look around I find I have taken not a single step. This is where I have always been.

In this light and airy house I am one and alone. My seeing God is the same as God seeing himself.

My true self is God, and God is the essence of all things. I see into the nature of every single thing in the world. In opening one door I have opened all.

6

God's simple essence is everywhere. He resides
in everything and yet he remains undivided. If
we find God we find him whole. This is how the
many become one.

7

To be full of myself is to have no room for God.
To make room for God I must be empty.

This emptiness is like a desert, a wild open country.
It is so still not even God moves here. God is still
and rests here. He gives up being God here.

In this place God is naked and concerns himself
with nothing but being.

8

Without form there is no change, without change there is no time. Our real nature is formless, changeless, apart from the passage of time: always this moment now. The events of last year are past, but our real nature of last year is now. The events of next year are future, but our real nature of next year is now.

9

One of the many names given to our nature is the Clear Light. The Clear Light is still in itself, but it is by this stillness that all things are moved, that the living receive life. God who is still becomes God who is active.

God's creativity has been likened to a dance: with his feet he dances the story of the universe, with his hands, demonstrating his love, he blesses.

10
Unity has two aspects: all things in essence are
the same Clear Light, united inwardly, and all
things are contained within the Clear Light,
united outwardly.

Once I see the truth of my own nothingness
and let go of everything, I find that everything
belongs to me, from the night sky to this smudge
of ink on my finger.

Seeing now with a clear eye, I notice how each
thing is so much itself. Everything within me –
that star, this hand – becomes charged with its
own existence.

11
We can be free from the restlessness of our
self-will by seeing and accepting our own inner
poverty. This is where we end and God begins.
We can abandon ourselves and trust in God's will.

Like the man who, each morning as he put on his
slippers, reminded himself that his day belonged
to God, we can see into the truth, day by day, and
find a steadiness.

12

The story of the world is the story of God. What is it all about? It is the story of how God gets to know himself.

He creates the world and ventures out of his home, taking on the disguise of whatever he meets. The door closes behind him, he forgets his home and loses himself in the world. If we think we are separate, if we think we are this and not that, we are God who has lost himself, God in disguise. If we find we are really whole, we are God come home.

God's fulfilment is in re-discovering his own identity. Nobody but God finds God. This is the the time when he lets himself go, and his heart leaps with joy. God is whole and God is aware.

All nature joins to celebrate God. Everything we look at points back to ourselves. When we are home we cease to feel alienated from the world, and enjoy instead a sense of friendliness with stones and trees, animals and people. We see into a truth which is wide and deep and astounding.

Seeing (1980)

for Simon and Kate

The Oneness Of Things

The sun low over the beach:
shining wires of dune grass,
stones and the shadows of stones.
On the shoreline, the rush of foam
mirrored in the wet sand.
In the oneness of things
I am nowhere in sight.

Marriage

(for Carole)

To see your face
with the eye of emptiness
is to have your face
as my own, and to find
between seeing and loving
not even a hairbreadth.

Five Haiku

Every flower in
        his first flower-smelling year
                is a daffodil.

Her book, held upside
        down, moves my daughter to sing
                in her loudest voice.

The thunderstorm passed,
        we run out in the warm air
                to gather hailstones.

Wheels spinning, we reach
        the hilltop – and this house
                lined with icicles.

As these stars answer
        a look with shivers of light –
                how deep the silence.

The Bull

(After Kuo-an)

The Search

In wild country, I part the tall grasses,
Endlessly looking out for the bull.
I follow rivers, not knowing their names,
Take trails deep into the mountains.
Who says I have already found the bull?
In the evening I sit exhausted,
Listening to the chirring of cicadas.

The Source

Only in imagination
Is my true nature lost.
It is the source
From which, alone, I watch
The endless changes.
The river flows from the mountain,
The willow bends to the water.

Birthday

The gale dying, cypresses on the bank
rock with the last gusts.

A bale hangs in the hedge,
water shudders along a wheel track.

My fingers hook into the rough bark
of logs I stack by the house.

My being is too airy to define
the particular feel of thirty years.

I stretch and listen to jackdaws
chacking in the cold March air.

Lights

At night I stand on the hill
above the town.
In a rainy tree a streetlight spins.
Lights in clusters across the valley
are brilliant in the rainswept air.
Abandoned, the road takes me down,
meandering,
deep with reflections.

Without Rift

Fields

As I walk in fields I chance
on an image a grey wraith
drifting over furrows stooping
to a stone its fingers pass through
and I fall in a glare unlearning
grey scarves come adrift wisping
into nothingness what am I now
an eye no body no mind
and sharpened like this hare
loping over furrows pausing
ears raised attentive to the wind.

Boundless

Like the wind searching,
lifting feathers round
the sparrow's neck,
lifting leaves in a wave
across the bean field,
I find no place
where I can say,
here my being ends.

River Trees

Down from the weir,
I cross the river on stepping stones.
My foot slips
and I wade knee deep
to the bank.

On the trunk of an elm
leaning over the water,
I lie back,
overwhelmed by the friendliness of trees.
Without rift,
how wide-eyed we are,
how lighthearted.

Pai-yang Mountains

A stream, slanted trees, then mist:
the mountains rise from nothing.
Up there its like Cold Mountain.

Pai-yang: the wind blows through you;
mist for your feet, mist for hands,
and for head the broad heaven.

Cornfield

When I paused
to look at an ear
of corn, tenderness
passed like a hand
across the field.

Mirror

Seeing no face where I am,
the one appearing in the mirror
is no double, but comes –
tonight again, the fascination –
like a face at the window.

Six Haiku

(For Malcolm and Maureen)

Under the glare
   of the station lights
the worn steps glitter.

In the tunnel
   the black taxi roof
   a stream of neon.

Sweetest by far,
   the first strawberry
      from the kitchen bowl.

Voices cross
 the stillness of the common –
rooks and men.

The moorhen's flurry –
 treading on it's own
  reflection.

Foghorn morning –
 cormorants dive apart,
  rise together.

In Fog

Something wild in the cat
I stroked on the doorstep
sent me walking in the fields.
Droplets from the fog
hang in the hedge.
I stand, my hand wet
from touching thorns,
and have no understanding.

Meadow

February after rain I wake
new to myself and see
everything alive stepping
into brilliant air
pitch black rooks great oak
felled by wind buzzing
with chainsaws smoke caught under
trees in bars of sunlight
wood's edge leaves curled brown
horse chestnut oak the meadow
white with snowdrops
and here I am I say here
I am looking up at cumulus
perfectly still.

The Zig-Zag Path

a cycle of poems

1   A Bag Of Stones

A gleam plummets,
　　there and not there,
　　and the stone goes down in the sea.
On the belly of the water the sunlight glitters.
It flits in a wave and glints among stones.
The boy hunches under the cliff.
He has clamped his jaw
　　and snarled up his cry inside.
His breath hisses as he stands
　　and pulls at the mouth of his bag.
He searches the beach for the stones.
Each one he picks is marked with a star.
Each has the dome of a skull.
He plunges his hand
　　as a wave sucks back
　　and catches a stone in its roll.
And when he stops his face is the mask of a sob.
He hoists the bag to his chest
　　and wraps his arms around it.

2   The Burial

Over the hill a black cloud sweeps,
   on the brow is a hole and a mound.
The rain cries down, the wind cries out.
He reaches down and again he reaches down.
Around the curled body he sets a ring of stones.
The wind flaps at the mouth of the bag.
His knees are stiff with kneeling.
His arm reaches around the mound
   and he drags the wet earth.
Slowly it crumbles, slurs and falls
   from the curve of his arm.
It falls over the stones, the cold skin
   and the turned away face.
The earth is blackened with rain,
   and under, under the earth, there is blackness.
He presses his hands down and stands,
   his dead weight bowed, and he has done.

3 His Wound Bleeds

He stumbles in darkness
   until the hill subsides
   and swallows him, dead but not dead.
He lies stiffly and his wound bleeds.
It bleeds and darkens the earth around.
And around him is a ring of stones.
They are stone hearts where his blood
   runs in little shudders.
The trickles are tiny cries in the earth.
His blood runs into the veins of the earth.
And he is wrapped in the red of a womb.
He is curled with the murmur of a heart,
   a child in the earth.

4   The New Cry

Something muscular pads inside the earth.
It trembles to touch him
    and it squeezes in close.
It nudges the water to flow
    over the lip and down.
It kneads and presses him to uncurl in the wake
    and it pushes him through.
Now the gentle air holds him
    and moves as he moves.
He peels the old skin from his body,
    slips it from his hands, and steps away.
And when he hears the new cry
    he listens enthralled.
It is his own cry caught on a ribbon of breath.
And when the night comes
    to clothe the green hollow
    his blood lullabies in his ears.

5 The Glade

The fat leaves buckle as he passes
    and brush him with their soft leathers.
The oak and the ash are poised.
Their heads are filled with intricacies.
Not one footfall cracks and explodes
    into wings and cries.
His breathing is the smallest wafting of air
    and a deer stands close and watches,
      its ear ticking in a shaft of light.
When he kneels at the pool the moss sighs.
His cupped hands break the water
    like a ghost melting into a mirror.
He drinks and the coolness threads inside him.
He bathes his face in transparency
    and he pours it over head and neck.
The water splashes back into rings.
And the rings run to the bank
    with little strands of light,
      and whisper to the roots.

6   A Boneless Dancer

An iridescent hill alive under a blue sky.
This is the haunt of dreams.
He comes to a pile of slates
    on an outcrop of rock,
      intrigued by the leafy patterns.
Inside, something wakes, disturbed.
The slates lift, slide and clatter.
He steps back and a cool wind
    breathes on his skin.
Nosing out, an animal crawls from the pile.
On its armour is a painted picture, human,
    a boneless dancer.
It heads off, its feet wet with paint.
On the rock there are footprints like drums.
And suddenly the breathing stops.
The birds fly down to the stones
    and the stones weigh
      on the eyelids of the hill.
And the hill is draped in silence.

7   He Sees His Mark

He opens the drawstring
    and the pouch of his self turns inside out.
He becomes the air.
His hands are like birds inside him.
He is cast with the net of seeing
    and falls on the rocks and crevices.
He cups the starling as it flies to the ground.
In the oak he creeps to the veins and lobes.
He touches the wings of the moth.
At the fire he drifts with the conversation,
    moving from face to face.
He catches the delicate sheen on eyelashes.
And when the deer run from the hunters
    he sweeps from the first to the last.
His hand is on the shaft.
He is the driving spear and the wound's blood.
His eye flares white and his head drops down.
And he kneels at the kill
    and rests his hand on the neck
    in sudden quiet.
In the cave the paint is stirred
    with blood from his member
    and the cup held to his lips.
He sucks and fills his cheeks.
He places his hand on the wall and blows.
And he sees his mark
    in the spatter of red
    in the light of the flames.

8   The Crag

In moonlight he stands below the eagle's beak.
The rocks around him huddle together
   with round backs mothering stillness.
His shadow glistens at the edge.
He takes the zig-zag path
   where knobs draw his hands upward
   and grooves draw his feet.
And at first light he sees the great space
   in the lap of the hills,
   and the sea far below.
He takes the star stone from his pocket
   and warms it in his palm.
His arm swings from the hip
   and pitches the stone into the air.
And a gleam plummets,
   there and not there,
   and the stone goes down in the sea.

Speaking Trees (1999)

Nine Poems For The Green Man

Oak

On a barren hill, in a sigh of wind,
the wild man wriggled his feet into the earth.
The whorls of his toes split open

and his roots wormed into the darkness.
Their noses sniffed for moisture,
twitched into channels and threaded down.

Tunnelers, mole tough, they scraped.
They muscled in for an earth grip,
tensing against the tug of the wind.

The wild man's legs chafed and wept.
They veined together and scarred.
His arms stiffened and jaws locked.

His pores burst into a sweat of buds.
They swelled, shed their scales
and thrust out their spindles,

branching into a crooked maze.
He was an open lung, a body of veins,
a barkskinned hand fingering the sky.

And his great heart, in one pulse,
unwrapped a profusion of leaves,
released a rain of emerald flowers.

Heartwood

Inside the oak,
    the wild man lived as a current
    singing in a million capillaries.
In the sheath of bark,
    he slid his arms from the boughs,
    his feet from the roots,
    and curled deep in the heartwood.

His fingers, flexing, hooked in a crevice.
They wedged and strained to split the wood.
A breeze funneled in,
    touched his grain
    and snapped him into skin and bone.
He edged through the gap
    and stepped to the ground.

The air ached in his lungs
    and his breath spilled in a cloud.
The droplets crackled into a glimmer of bees.
They spun in a daze to the tree.
He climbed to a bough,
    touched the soft moss
    in the dells of the bark,
    and was stilled.

River

The sunlit river was a mirror.
The wild man's tears fell
from the sky down to the sky.

Teardrops flashed into dragonflies
skitting to the tips of reeds.

Teardrops inflated to frogs
kicking into widening circles.

Teardrops stretched into minnows
nibbling at the stems of weeds.

Teardrops roiled the mud,
rising as little fists of water-lily
to open their palms.

Teardrops spotted a pad,
rushing from splayed feet
into startled moorhen.

She stepped away, with a flick
of her tail, and was gone.

Moon Stories

1
The wolf, the moon heavy in her belly,
padded on pine needles.
On a ridge, in darkness, she retched.
With a surge the moon grazed her fangs
and rolled into the sky.
Quivering, bereft, she howled in its wake.

2
The whale sleeping on the wide sea
woke to the moon
running in silver to her eye.
Her mouth gaped and she gulped
a booming seafall.
The sea drained down, streaking the beaches.
Starfish squirmed, anemones
drew in their tentacles.

3
The owl in the wood was blinded by moonlight.
Her neck ruffled and she hooted,
casting darkness from her beak.
It fell in silence through the branches,
settling under leaves and the ears of fungus.
Under the ferns of the wood,
like black snow, the shadows fell.

4

The wild man meandered through the night.
Roots and slender stems with leafy twigs
threaded from his mouth.
He dug with his hands and tenderly
planted the saplings,
tamping the soil at their roots.
He moved over the brown earth,
stepping lightly, speaking trees.

Trees

The hazel stood in a bush,
cobnuts in their frilly skirts
curtsying to the breeze.

The hawthorn hid under froth,
a white bouquet,
like milk poured from a pail.

The alder perched by the river
with scaly feet clutching,
ruffling its leafy hearts.

The sallow had springy branches
like young goats chased by bees,
tails waving goodbye.

Blossom

The blue tit flitted
    in the cherry tree
showering blossom.

Scents

(For Hagar Francis, 1882–1974)

The child tilted its head to the breast,
nose gliding on the scent.

The hay lifted the child high,
as on horseback, above meadows of sweetness.

Honeysuckle gently gripped the nape
and pulled the head down to fragrance.

The bucket's pock as it hit the well water
sounded the depth of damp leaf air.

Mushrooms in an earthy stir
opened little springs in the hollow of the mouth.

Lavender wafted a dreamy stream
fluttering in the nostrils and closing the eyes.

Firestone

A cracked flint revealed the gleam
of stone, nestling in the palm.
It was a door: knocked on, it unlocked fire.

It struck up the glitter of dust motes,
the sparkle of wings.

It spat out the flare of jack-o-lanterns,
the shimmer of streams.

Storm nut with a flame kernel,
it hung in a black cloud.
Mirror of lightning, it rained in a blaze.

It split trees and kindled a radiance.
It rolled from embers or blackened
under mounds of ash.

A small egg that broke with a flicker
to dazzle and scorch.
A sky gift, hatching heaven's fire.

Sanctuary

The wild man hid by a gravestone,
bent low in the shadow of yew.

He flattened his hands and pressed
his forehead to the cobbled wall.
They sank, his head and shoulders
disappeared into the masonry,
like leaning on a screen of water.

His face entered a carved mask,
his cheeks fitting into cheeks,
nose breathing through stone nostrils.
Blind eyes opened and the wild man
peered into the nave.

Shafts of light cast shawls
over the stone and rinsed the air
in underwater blues and greens.
He saw the dark brilliance of wood,
the polished flow of grain whirling into knots.

A carved mouse on a benchend
twitched its tail to vine and barley
in a chiselled sheaf.
A bear nodded in a roundel,
a hare crouched with flattened ears.

Pillars of stone grew like oaks,
branching into a timber vault,
a maze of traceries.
Christ slumped on a wooden cross,
head bent, crowned with bramble.

Candles in a quiver kept the fire.
Framed in a shield, a woodwose stiffened,
his club like a swollen fist.
At his feet, a jar of violets
stood on a sliver of glassy light.

The wild man peered, not moving
a muscle, leaning on the silence.

CPSIA information can be obtained
at www.ICGtesting.com
Printed in the USA
LVHW030334110520
654944LV00007B/939